FACE IT & FINISH IT

FACE
IT
&
FINISH
IT

WRITTEN BY:

TERRENCE SANI

FACE IT
IT

FINISH
IT

YOUR STRUGGLE IS SMALLER THAN YOUR ABILITY TO SUCCEED

TERRENCE SANI

YOU ARE YOUR OUTCOME

THE ROAD TO SUCCESS IS HIGHLY FLAMMABLE

THIS BOOK IS DEDICATED TO:

Any individual who holds a burning desire and grinds for an opportunity but lacks the ability to see past his or her various walls.

The *Freethinker's* and truth seekers once like myself who've joined multiple accountability groups, masterminds, attended seminars, bought the recommended books from the so-called "guru's", accepted an offer in exchange for an email address, invested in a business or "life coach" and are **STILL stuck.**

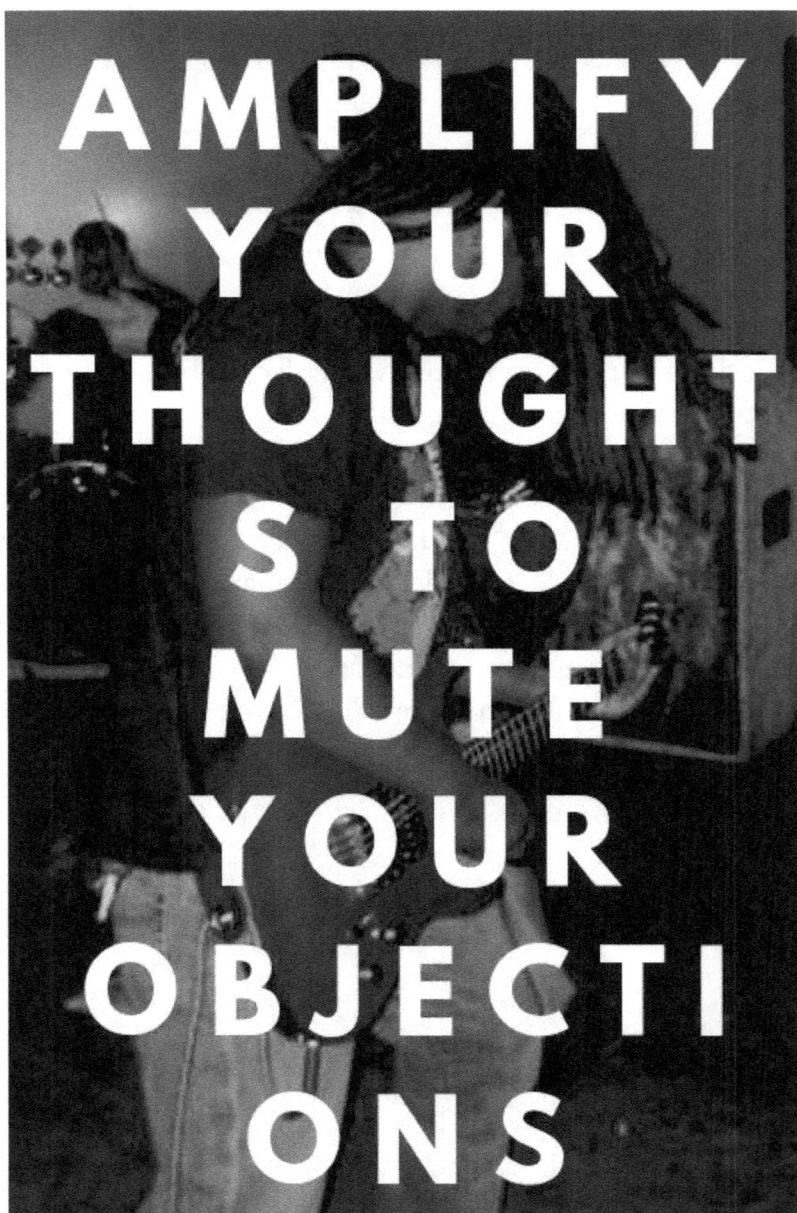

AMPLIFY YOUR THOUGHTS TO MUTE YOUR OBJECTIONS

SUCCESS IS:

The ability to look behind you and see what you've accomplished, to look ahead and see what you've yet to penetrate.. all while moving forward because you refuse to stand still.

WHAT DOES SUCCESS MEAN TO YOU?

_____

_____

_____

_____

YOU'RE FLUENT IN YOUR EXCUSES BUT YOUR GREATNESS IS A FOREIGN LANGUAGE

TERRENCE SANI - 10

YOUR PATH YOUR DESTINATION

IF YOUR EFFORTS EXHAUST YOUR RESULTS, YOU MAY BE ASKING THE RIGHT PEOPLE THE WRONG QUESTIONS

ACKNOWLEDGEMENTS

I'd like to acknowledge the trampoline that sat in my family's backyard for a few months until I decided to **face** the laziness and **finish** the job that would result in the happiness displayed on my kid's **face**s.

I'd like to thank **Ermias Asghedom** a.k.a. Nipsey Hussle. Even though I don't know you personally. 70% of this book was written while listening to your music. I've significantly respected your progressive business and personal development strategies. I aim to one day say thank you to you **face** to **face**.

Finally, I'd like to acknowledge you the reader who may not be where you currently feel you should. Know that the life you live can indeed match your vision, after reading this book I hope that you can finally create the lens to see the big picture.

*I wrote the acknowledgements to this book less than 24 hours before Nipsey Hussle was murdered. I struggled but decided to leave my "thank you" as is. Your struggle is smaller than your ability to succeed. #TheMarathonContinues

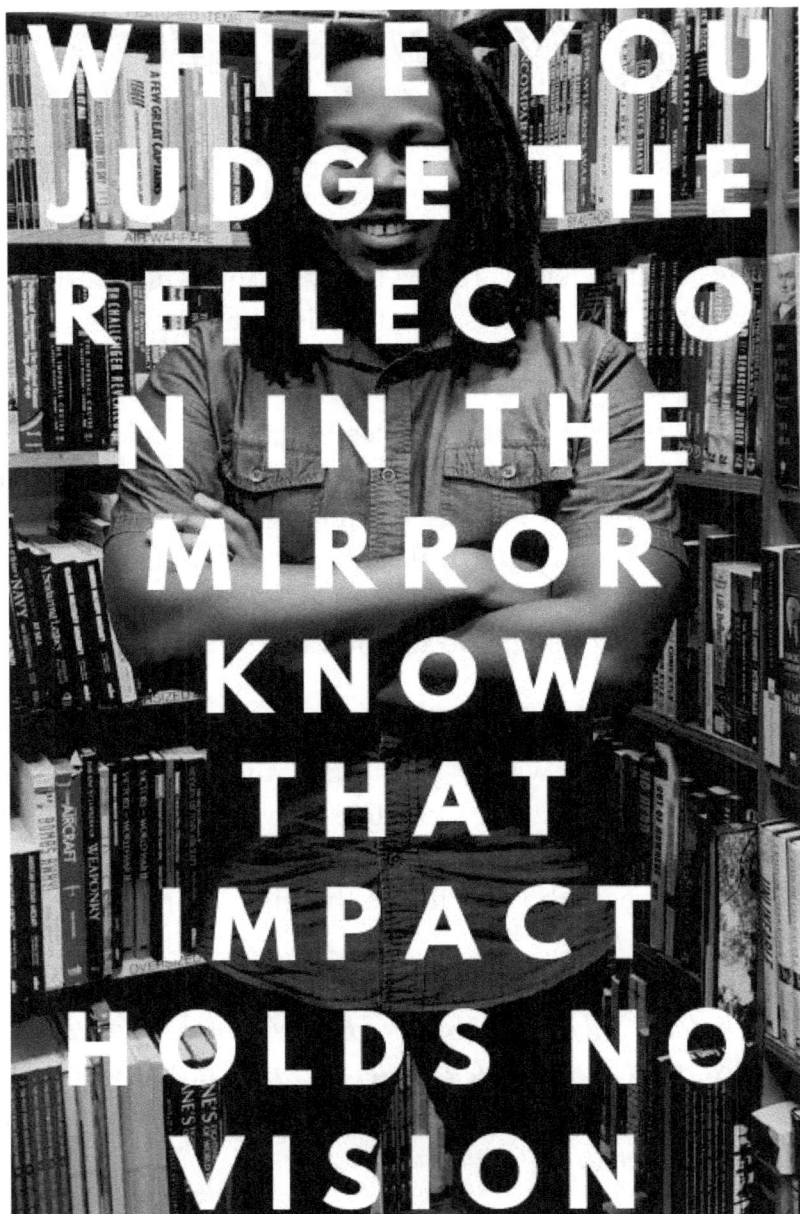

WHILE YOU
JUDGE THE
REFLECTIO
N IN THE
MIRROR
KNOW
THAT
IMPACT
HOLDS NO
VISION

TERRENCE SANI – 14

How to use this book!

THE CONCEPT IS A SIMPLE 3 STEP PROCESS:

1. Plant
2. Nurture
3. Harvest

PLANTING: TERRENCE'S TAKEAWAYS

This follows the end of every chapter, extracting major key points, stories and concepts I have personally selected for you.

NURTURE: YOUR TAKEAWAYS

Did something hit home from the chapter that specifically resonated with you?

HARVEST: WHAT WILL YOU FACE & FINISH?

Reading the information is only half the work, it's time to take action!

THE ANTI-INTRODUCTION

Hopefully, you've purchased this book not only because of the handsome guy on the cover but also due to an unresolved issue you're currently having. When I was a kid I once saw an episode of Garfield and Friend's, where Garfield made a short-sided comment regarding the ridiculousness of all the subscription cards that still came in magazines even after he had already subscribed to the magazine. I personally share a similar feeling when it comes to the introduction of books.

Sure an introduction or forward from a highly respected celebrity would make this book a tad bit thicker and perhaps give my brand *You Are Your Outcome* a little more credibility. But how will that help *you* the reader succeed? Often in life, we default to such unnecessary or irrelevant ordeals. My point is not all the time but often introductions in books aren't always necessary. I don't like "fluff" and I doubt you do either.

When you go out on a date you spend time making moments, creating history and getting to know each other. You aren't exactly prepped to know specifically

what you're getting yourself into ahead of time. You **FACE** it. When you go out to a restaurant, on average you aren't typically informed about the history of the meal that eventually became an option on your menu. You came to eat!

You don't need to be prepped for this book. Now I know many people like to get their feet wet and test the water first, as opposed to just jumping right on in. That's probably what you've grown accustomed to and may very well be the reason why you picked this up. However, this book is called *Face It Finish It*. So let's dive right in.

SUCCESS HAS AN INVOICE, IT'S THE TRUTH. BUT IT'S HARDER TO PAY IF YOU'RE ENSLAVED BY DEEP ROOTS.

TERRENCE SANI - 18

CHAPTER 1
BREAKING THE SEAL

"If your excuses outweigh your actions, you might be mentally out of shape."

A surplus of effort can overcome a deficit of opportunity. Years ago I didn't know where I was going, but the one thing I was sure of was that my life had to get better and that I was tired of where I was residing mentally, physically and financially.

As usual, I didn't have a guide to help me out. So I sought advice from other people. Feeling as if I needed the approval to go out and put myself in a better situation to not merely exist but to actually live. I spent many years wasting a lot of money and time trying to find the perfect answer, business plan, vibe and language that would help feed me the information in such a digestible manner that would somehow magically get me to where I'd like to be.

Let me give you a piece of advice I doubt anyone will ever throw at you: If you want to educate yourself on something new, as in something you yourself haven't yet experienced. Do not default to the internet and simply use it as your first go-to source for answers. In fact, try to make it your last resource. Why? Because the internet is littered with sketchy and non-credited information. It's like trying to self-diagnose yourself via Google. While you may currently reside in a trial and error phase on your journey to success, so may be the self-proclaiming expert or leader that you currently follow.

People can throw you "game" or give you advice, they can even go a step further and mentor or coach you. But I promise you, nobody's voice will ever be as loud or hold as much weight as your very own. Don't wait for someone to give you the "green light". The permission to take action can only come from within.

Now let's say you have been waiting on that ever so holy green light and it presents itself in whatever shape or form. Then what? What's next? What good is a sign without action? Acknowledging the sign alone isn't effective. Why not? Because just as life, success is give and take and if there's nothing for you to sacrifice on your end at all then you're just a spectator. You'll see the sign but seeing it alone doesn't put you in a position to receive anything but a vision or idea.

Understand you don't have to wait for a sign, you don't have to wait for anything. Let's keep things 100% real. Waiting is honestly just comfortable for you, which is why you default to that. You have things you need to get done, goals to accomplish, money to make and you're seriously just waiting for a sign?

Listen, I will provide no green lights throughout this book. Why? Because you have to be the one to make the next move. As always, my intention is to expose the ideas that force you to take action on your goals. But it's you my friend that holds the weight and ability to create the motion and momentum.

As always you've been in front of every action and thought you've ever had or made so how could you ever follow anyone? Ask yourself, who's really leading you? Who's really following the leader? The excess weight you're holding onto is hindering your opportunity. Stop looking for the perfect tools, apps, mentors, accountability groups, journals or attending the same old dry seminars. Trust me I've done it all and it will deter you from your purpose.

You don't need the same thing everyone else needs. We all know the importance of a strong foundation but don't spend the rest of your life trying to find the perfect spot to plant your seed in the soil. This book will help you obtain the fertilizer for sustainable growth. But it will not plant the seed for you. What you need to realize is that success is in the palm of your hand, you control its weight and proportion by taking action so if it gets heavy and falls or simply blows away in the wind, know that it's got your name attached to it.

Back when I was a personal trainer I told people, "I don't care how much you can lift, I workout with the weight the world puts on my shoulders." There is no external gatekeeper for success. You'll find that it's much harder to remove yourself from an old conditioned habit if you never take the shot but always pass the ball to the person you see as the most valuable player on the team.

Here's something crazy for you to digest. My senior year of high school I was asked out to the homecoming dance by one of if not the most beautiful girl in our senior class, Chrisalee. Do you think I took her up on her offer? Nope, like the coward I was I wrote her a dumb sappy letter justifying how I wasn't worthy and how she deserved to go with someone else. Yes, I really did that. Of course now in retrospect, this is completely self-defeating and something I'd never do.

As an only child living in a single parent household, the only "romantic" relationship characteristics I came across to learn from were on tv. Hence me putting women on pedestals they never deserved and placing them so high that I couldn't ever meet them there myself, or so I thought. Regardless of if you think my denial reason was sweet or ridiculous, do you think it hindered Chrisalee from going to our homecoming dance in any way, shape, or form? Hell no! Of course not, she went with someone else.

If you've ever worked in any customer service field dealing with an older demographic, you'll come to realize there's a diminishing need for them to filter any verbal communication whatsoever. Their mouths are just as controllable as their bladder and I'm sure I'll be the same way when I'm older.

For us humans, there's always assistance with baby deliveries into the world. With our daughter Norah, the doctor manually broke the sack to start the delivery process.

Ever watch a snake, crocodile or chicken break through its shell? The shell is nothing but an outside barrier that provides temporary protection. After time, suddenly the animal or reptile starts to poke through the walls in which it lives in. Once it's able to break free it's time to take on the world. If there's one thing we can all agree on, let's agree that we as humans are meant to progress.

TRY THIS EXERCISE:

WHEN YOU WAKE UP AND GET READY TO MAKE SOMEONE ELSE MONEY AND BEFORE YOU GO OUT AND ALLOW SOMEONE TO DETERMINE HOW MUCH YOU'RE WORTH...

I WANT YOU TO TRY THIS SIMPLE EXERCISE OUT FOR A _WEEK_ THAT'S _SEVEN_ STRAIGHT DAYS.

EVERY MORNING WHEN YOU FIRST WAKE UP, WRITE DOWN ON A SCALE OF 1-10 HOW MOTIVATED YOU ARE:
- To do great things
- To be a part of something great
- To do what you actually love

ONE OF TWO THINGS WILL HAPPEN:
1. You'll realize how comfortable you are at lying to yourself.
2. You'll become aware of the things you don't like and take action to remove them.

If Cardi B's song *"Bodak Yellow"* moves you more than your purpose does. You my friend, have some reevaluating to do.

Have you ever watched one of those shows on HGTV, where they flip houses? They turn a house that most would want to leave alone into a dream home.

As dysfunctional as the house may appear to be physically or visually, it can't repair itself. The interiors usually have to be gutted out and demolished. When I was in high school my part-time job was to go help my dad remodel houses, restaurants and other business establishments.

Every day we watch these shows and are blown away in disbelief by the before and after images. We're amazed at how they took a house from nothing to something. We see the result of the interior designer's imagination but don't realize we're actually designers ourselves.

We all have walls but you also have options. You can grab a large sledgehammer and start to demolish the walls of your comfort zone, grab a regular sized hammer to nail down bad choices and habits or lastly, decorate the walls of your comfort zone with your favorite excuses.

Obstacles are often like bullies, they don't go away until after you've put your foot down and shown it who's boss. You'll be surprised with the things that back down in life once you decide to step up. Most people would rather not be in situations where they consistently have to go **face** to **face** against someone that has the ability and fearlessness to get back up after being knocked down each and every single time.

I'll break this down for you even more: Netflix, Hulu, Disney+ or whatever subscription-based service utility bill that makes its way to you. The reason why you pay it is because you've agreed to the terms and conditions. I say that to say this. Who's agreeing to your terms? Have you set your own boundaries?

There's a movie by Bruce Lee titled "The Big Boss". After having a troubled past Bruce moves away from his environment and moves in with relatives. He's then given a jade necklace and makes a vow to never fight or cause trouble anymore. Throughout the first quarter of the movie, he's tested and put in all kinds of situations in which most people would break their vow or engage in a physical altercation. But after numerous attempts of trying to be the mediator and peacemaker, his necklace was accidentally ripped off and the jade had shattered onto the ground. Then all hell broke loose. The jade necklace was a representation of his vow, but once broken all was fair game.

Do you understand how a "vow" works? A vow is a promise, something that shall not be broken. The good thing about a vow is its weight. Solidifying and abiding by your vows can save you money, time, frustration and possibly even your life. Would it be a stretch to even say vows are safety nets? I'd like to think not but I can't help but wonder. Vows have the ability to affect your relationships, environment, habits, and lifestyles. Vows can make sure you're at the right place at the right time and with the right people. Almost five years ago I made a vow to stop eating meat and I haven't looked back since. Why? Because the weight of my vow greatly exceeds a mere thought or desire for eating meat.

Putting your foot down doesn't have to be negative. But you do need to set your mark and provide a line that does not ever need to be crossed.

Examples of putting your foot down:
- Agreeing to never go five days or so without calling a loved one/friend
- Refusing to go a single day without prospecting clients for your business
- Removing any one of your social media friends that lack a progressive direction

TERRENCE'S TAKEAWAY

WHAT YOU SEE ISN'T ALWAYS WHAT YOU GET, BECAUSE YOU DON'T GET ANYTHING TANGIBLE UNTIL YOU TAKE ACTION.

IF YOUR EXCUSES OUTWEIGH YOUR ACTIONS, YOU MIGHT BE MENTALLY OUT OF SHAPE. JUST BECAUSE YOU MAY HOLD YOURSELF BACK DOESN'T MEAN SOMEONE ELSE WILL.

PLAYING A GAME OF COMPARE AND CONTRAST WITH YOUR SHOULDA, COULDA WOULDA'S IS LIKE PLAYING HOPSCOTCH IN QUICKSAND.

WE DON'T LACK CREATIVITY, PEOPLE CREATE FEAR EVERY DAY BUT IF WE CAN CREATE FEAR WHO'S TO SAY WE CAN'T CREATE AN OPPORTUNITY?

IF PEOPLE ARE TAKING ADVANTAGE OF YOU, PERHAPS IT'S BECAUSE YOU'VE GIVEN THEM THE PATHWAY. PUT YOUR FOOT DOWN AND LET YOUR OBSTACLES SPIT SHINE YOUR SHOES!

IF YOU'RE HELPING SOMEONE LIVE THE LIFE YOU LACK, WHAT ARE YOU RECEIVING IN RETURN?

YOUR TAKEAWAYS:

WHAT WILL YOU FACE & FINISH?

I DON'T CARE IF YOU GOTTA BUILD A FOUNDATION ON ROCKY WATER, LEARN HOW TO FLOAT.

CHAPTER 2
AN OPPORTUNITY COST

"If you're comfortable where you are, you'll never be equipped for anything better."

Have your parent's ever made you wash your mouth out with soap for saying bad words? Well, things never got that bad for me. Or so I thought.. but as the years went by in my life I realized the older I got the filthier my mouth became. If you tell people your job sucks what does that say about you? If you say your spouse is "too much work" what does it say about you? You may hate paying bills, but I bet you enjoy the pleasure of having what you're being billed for, right?

Sometimes your thoughts are light but your words are very heavy. When you complain you're simply exposing your flaws, absent-mindedness and a lack of ability to see that you're not without lingering incapabilities either.

Why are we more likely to not only do what we hate, but consistently do it? Stick to your goal, it's more important to address the distraction or obstacle head on than to pay the cost of comfort. Ever ask someone how their day was going, only for them to gloat about themselves and never ask you how your own day went? They talk about themselves so much that they naturally dismiss the thought of ever throwing the question back at you.

Belief in the truth becomes much more difficult to dispute when you've experienced specific situations. What sense does it make attempting to figure out how things are going to go wrong? Why aren't you concerned with how you can progress and make things better instead? If you're comfortable where you are, you'll never be equipped for anything better.

I hear so many entrepreneurs and speakers talk about getting to the "next level". Do you have any idea what your "next level" is? You gotta be careful because sometimes we associate levels with rewards. Your next level is just another chapter to the book of your life. Your next level is just confirmation that your previous mission is over and that your next mission has started, it's another grind, another challenge NOT a reward.

DOES THIS SOUND FAMILIAR?
1. You buy a book from a successful author.
2. The book is about how to be successful.
3. You **finish** the book but you aren't much further in success than you were from the start.

Isn't it crazy how you can move forward yet still be in the same place? Who's the sucker? Who got fooled?

Everyone wants to eat the food, gather around the dinner table when it's time to eat but nobody wants to take action on the recipe, nobody wants to go to the store, buy the ingredients or go in the kitchen and cook.

STEPS COME BEFORE LEVELS

You gotta learn to crawl before you run. At the time this book was written, our youngest child Norah was only a year old. She had several steps (Pun intended) before she could get from point A to point B.

First, she had to know which direction she wanted to go, crawl, pull herself up, stand up, take steps and walk, then finally run.

We usually think about what we can receive before what we can offer. Do you stop eating when you're full or do you **finish** everything that's in front of you until it's gone? Do you feel sluggish, sleepy and tired afterward? I have, plenty of times and I want you to know there is no difference between that and comfort. You go to the same job, you do the same thing, get paid the same and complain about the same issues (usually to the same people who are doing the same thing as you). What's the one thing that has the possibility to change everything? YOU, you have the potential to change each and every aspect of your life.

Ever go grocery shopping when you're hungry? You

instantly become careless. All you see is an opportunity. You'll start creating mental recipes on the spot! By the time you get home you regret all of the unnecessary crap you didn't plan on buying. Here's another example, what about when you need to go to the restroom and you can't. You start dancing, moonwalking, pop locking, pacing back and forth. It's like you've been hooked up to a Red Bull I.V. you just can't stay still.

Many of us are very "sur**face**" with our actions. We want to be entrepreneurs but we take the standard external approach: attending seminars, networking, online courses, business cards or even building websites. But the internal things remain hidden: no product, no client, no experience, no problems people can pay you to solve.

Think about what you're attracted to and what you'd do for free anyway. Ask yourself does it set you apart? If not, what can you do to put your own spin on things?

OVERINDULGING

Recently I went to a local hole in the wall Chinese food restaurant (Timmy Chan's for all you mutual Houstonian's), I hadn't been there in ages. But I self willingly overindulged, so much to the point where I had to hold onto a shopping cart because I was having dizzy spills hours later in the fruit section of a grocery store! (Probably due to the salt)

Just as always I tried to figure out the life lesson in this. Many of us get really excited about our intentions. So much that we overindulge in information we can't always process in just one sitting. The last thing you want is an overload of information you can't do anything with. My first book, *You Are Your Outcome* wasn't formatted to read from beginning to end.

Many of us can read a great story but come up short, without any real life actionable takeaways. That book was designed to be a "go to" tool. If you can't get a grip on the lessons you learn, you'll mismanage them.

Every short section of that book places you in a position to **face** the obstacle so that you have just enough information to retain and take action.

I had so many books on my shelf just collecting dust, I didn't know where to start with them so I banned myself (with the help of my wife) from buying books for an ENTIRE YEAR!

YOU WORK SO HARD DOING SO MANY THINGS THAT WHEN THE OPPORTUNITY COMES YOU AREN'T PREPARED. HOW DO YOU RESOLVE THIS??

1. Take your time
2. Take action
3. Write things down

Let's say for example that you want a pair of Jordans, you can look at a picture in a magazine a million times but you won't get any closer to them being on your feet. If you focus so much on what you want, you'll miss out on the steps to actually get it. You can look at your bank account a million times but the numbers won't move until you move first.

Ever find some money on the ground? It means nothing until you decide to pick it up, the value is literally ZERO until you take action.

What you have is good enough, what you have is exactly what you need for right now. When I had my first book expo I had no banner, custom tablecloth, t-shirts, flyers or bookmarks. All I had was a book and a bookstand, but I managed to sell books every single hour. Nobody cared about my brand at first, in fact my book was double the price of the surrounding books that authors were selling around me.

Now one might think I backed myself into a corner, but please understand I didn't sell people on just the book. I sold bridges, my goal was to bridge the gap between the problem and the purpose. My customers bought bridges not books, therefore I strongly suggest you inquire bridging the gap to greatness.

YOU BRING ABOUT WHAT YOU COMPLAIN ABOUT.

YOU'RE WHERE YOU ARE BASED ON WHAT YOU HAVEN'T YET DONE.

PERFECTION IS A CRIME AND YOU'VE GOT FINGERPRINTS ALL OVER IT. DON'T ALLOW YOUR MIND TO ARREST YOUR ABILITY TO EXECUTE.

IF YOU STRUGGLE THINKING OUTSIDE THE BOX IT'S MOST LIKELY BECAUSE YOU'RE FOCUSED ON WRAPPING THE PACKAGE.

IF YOU WAIT TOO LONG TO TAKE ACTION YOU RISK BEING FORCED TO FACE AN UNCOMFORTABLE SITUATION.

YOU DON'T HAVE TO REINVENT THE WHEEL BUT YOU CAN CONTROL THE DIRECTION, SPEED, DURATION AND WHAT THE WHEEL IS ATTACHED TO.

YOU CAN'T BUILD ANYTHING BY PLAYING HOT POTATO.

YOUR TAKEAWAYS:

WHAT WILL YOU FACE & FINISH?

DON'T SIGN UP TO GET THE TOOLS, IF YOU DON'T KNOW WHAT YOU'RE BUILDING

TERRENCE SANI – 42

CHAPTER 3
EVALUATE THE PROBLEM

"Your absence is making the money that belongs in your bank account."

If you're anything like me you've been suckered into believing "secrets" whether it be video, book or magazine.

WHAT SECRETS AM I REFERRING TO?

- The **unbelievable secret** to losing weight
- The **lost secret** to creating passive income
- The **biggest secret** to quitting your job
- The **never before seen secrets** to health
- The **untold secrets** of wealth
- The **unknown secrets** to love
- The **hidden secrets** of finding real..
  (I'll stop myself here)

If success was a legit secret, then why are so many people obtaining it every day? Why are more and more individuals dropping out of college and building successful businesses?

My favorite speaker Les Brown, considered one of if not the best speaker in the world, has delivered roughly the same speech in its entirety for decades. Every time I've seen him I've known 90% of what was going to come out of his mouth. There's no secret to what he does because he's been doing it for years. He's created something so original and authentic that he can repeatedly inspire, impact, and get paid.

It's like going against Mike Tyson in his prime, you've seen him train, you've seen him knock people out. You know what's gonna happen, you know what the result is going to be. The true question you need to ask yourself is what are you going to do about it? Don't allow your mind to see "obstacles" and automatically start seeing problems, see obstacles and start seeing solutions. Take some time to think about this, everything you currently love in this world has always been exposed and never hidden.

Maybe I'm a little bipolar (aren't we all). But I've decided to start looking at "absence" as another person. I'll explain...

If you spend most of your day working, doing something you absolutely don't love who's spending time with your loved ones?
YOUR ABSENCE IS!!!

Who's on an island sipping margaritas and reflecting on life?
YOUR ABSENCE IS!!!

YOUR ABSENCE
is making the money that belongs in your bank account.

YOUR ABSENCE
lives full and wants to die empty.

YOUR ABSENCE
is comfortable being around your kids, so after a while, they don't ask for <u>you</u> anymore.

Everything that you need and want is waiting for you to show up but..
YOU'RE ABSENT!!!

Your dreams, purpose, passion, and profits are doing roll call right now and
YOU'RE ABSENT!!!

Who's in the house you deserve???
YOUR ABSENCE IS

AT THE END OF THE DAY ASK YOURSELF:
1. Is absence where I currently want to be?
2. Do I have too many leaky faucets?
3. What in my life is irreplaceable?

MAKING YOUR PURPOSE PRESENT
One day we noticed what had appeared to be a mosquito bite on our son Hendrix's neck. It didn't

seem to be defined at all so we didn't think much of it and just moved on. As the days went by, his neck started looking kinda odd.. as if something was swollen and so we'd feel around it but again we thought it was still nothing to be serious about. Thinking maybe it would simply go away on its own. I'd poke and push it and he'd seem fine, jumping off sofas and trampolines just as normal toddlers do.

Typical remedies such as calamine lotion didn't help therefore letting us know that whatever this thing was, it apparently had no intention of going away. We took him in to see his pediatric doctor to evaluate it. (A great guy that I've personally coined "Passive Patterson") As many physicians do, he simply provided an antibiotic and said it should go away after a few days. About a week went by and not only was the mass on our son's neck more defined, but it was now also painful to the touch! It eventually got to the point where you could stand behind him and see a bulge coming from his neck.

We finally scheduled an appointment with the ENT. Unfortunately, Hendrix hadn't even turned two so he wasn't really talking much, which made things a bit worse being that he couldn't clearly describe his discomfort.

The next day at work my wife called saying it seemed like it had grown bigger overnight and that it was more firm than it had ever been. So I left work to go meet the family in the emergency room. After finally being seen, images were obviously needed and we're warned about his exposure to radiation at such a young age but what options did we really have? With the X-ray done, ultrasound done, CT scan done, and deductible now met. The ENT reviewed the CT scan and it turned out our son had a golf ball sized abscess next to his throat and would have to have surgery.

Surgery? Our son wasn't even two! All my life I've worked in healthcare, from psych wards, county hospitals and cancer centers where children just like little Hendrix die. As many patient charts as I've come across I would have never thought our son would be one of them. Not for something so serious. You never feel the full impact of these things until something hits home.

One-year-olds aren't supposed to go under the knife, one-year-olds aren't supposed to have surgery. Sure I've seen children on the news and in magazines but this wasn't supposed to happen to Hendrix, not our child. That's exactly what I kept telling myself. It was quite odd that we never saw the actual doctor while in the ER nor did we ever see the imaging results ourselves. It was a bad game of telephone through the nurse, which was the only person he decided to report to. After the ER doctor saw Hendrix's images he told the nurse that he could not perform surgery on our son due to the fact he had a rather complicated abscess.

A big mass with small masses around it and the fact that it was extremely close to his throat didn't help. At first, I was upset I asked myself how does this doctor call himself a doctor? Why was he working in the Emergency Room of all places? How could he carry that name MD? How could he consider himself a "specialist"?

Then I started to calm down and realized that if he wasn't confident in his ability to justify the hard work that got him to the level he's at, then he damn sure didn't need to cut open my son. He referred us to another surgeon so Hendrix had to get in an ambulance and was rushed downtown to Houston's famous medical center. Finally, we meet the surgeon. I don't think you heard me.. I said we MET the surgeon.. we saw him **face** to **face**, no middleman no nurse assistant or practitioner. He sat down with us and reassured us that this was not only common, but something he had treated many other times before and guaranteed us Hendrix would be alright.

This surgeon's outlook, confidence, and knowledge ran circles around the previous surgeon. So my question to you is what are you running circles around? Is something currently running circles around you?

TERRENCE'S TAKEAWAY

IT ISN'T HARD WORK THAT JUSTIFIES SUCCESS, IT'S RESILIENCY THAT ELIMINATES MEDIOCRITY.

IF SOMEONE TELLS YOU "NO", PERHAPS IT'S BEST TO APPRECIATE THE FACT THAT THEY DIDN'T SAY YES.

NEVER ALLOW OBSTACLES TO USE YOU AS AN ASSISTANT.

WHAT DO YOU DO WHEN YOUR "GO-TO SOURCE" FAILS?

YOUR TAKEAWAYS:

WHAT WILL YOU FACE & FINISH?

IF THERE'S A SUCH THING AS A SECRET TO SUCCESS, WHY ARE PEOPLE OBTAINING IT EVERYDAY?

CHAPTER 4
EVALUATE THE REWARD

"It's the process that makes things wonderful."

There are certain environments we don't allow babies and children into because we know it's not best for them, it's not healthy and it's detrimental to their development.

CAN YOU DEPEND ON YOU TO GET THE JOB DONE?

The reason why you aren't where you want to be is due to the fact that you refuse to see an obstacle as an opportunity. Until you **face** it you'll always be held back and you'll never **finish** the mission of getting what you know you deserve. Perhaps you don't know what you deserve, so let's take a quick step back.

Let's keep it 100, we often give up or run away from problems. What's crazy is mentally running away from a situation is almost effortless. It's comfortable! You don't need sneakers, you don't need to stretch (Ever pull a hamstring avoiding a mental setback?), you don't sweat and you can do it all from the comfort of your own mind.

FACING FATHERHOOD

For twelve long years, I went around a specific

problem. While refusing to meet this obstacle, I acquired the habit of taking shortcuts. Nobody taught me that shortcuts come with side effects. Well.. maybe someone did tell me, but I refused to listen. I actually spent more time avoiding situations than I did trying to resolve them.

I acquired bad habits and also taught myself how to look for loopholes in life, I learned how to do everything I could to not suffer even if it took more work to be fake and artificial.

No matter how much I hated my dad, no matter how deep I tried to bury my feelings and memories I couldn't help but think of him each and every Father's Day at least once. As a father myself, it was my responsibility to not only take notice but I had to take action and realize that I was being selfish.

I was allowing one hurdle to affect every area of my life. Ever see the movie Venom? Venom is a villain from Marvel Comics, an alien parasite or symbiote that attaches itself to its prey. You see when you get so emotionally involved as to actually "hate" something or someone, you unintentionally and unconsciously become what you hate.

I invited everything I disliked about my relationship with my father into my being, my home, my thoughts, voice, and actions. I was a monster. I was really short with my mom. My anger was bad with my wife I even punched a hole in the wall in front of her and our son. Our oldest Hez would scream "stop" when his mother and I verbally got into it.

Was I ever going to give my mom the quality time she deserved? Was I ever going to get my anger towards my wife under control? Was I ever going to be the best father possible to our kids? What was I teaching? What if our kids followed in my footsteps? If I couldn't **face** my father how the hell are my kids going to have the confidence to **face** the world?

You see, I could never give our family the best of me because I never resolved the negative feelings about my father. Maybe I thought I did, but I was a living resurrection of his presence. If you stay holding onto the problem you usually take full custody of the issue with stunted growth.

I knew I had to change so I ended the grudge so that I could be great in all areas of my life. Twelve years of pain and frustration was nothing but dead weight I was carrying. While that weight held me back I had to realize on my own why I was sluggish with my affections and actions. It's a lot harder to see the problem when you've become everything you dislike. I was a walking taking hypocrite. It took well over a decade to realize as long as I held that grudge I could only be as good as the problem. I could only be as good to my son's as my dad was to me, that's what I used to think.

Sure I may have physically been there but was I 100% emotionally invested? I always had a distraction, I always felt incapable. As a child my dad wasn't putting me to bed, he wasn't concerned with my grades, he didn't even know how to spell my name! Once he wrote a check out to me for rent and asked if my name was spelled with an "A" or not. (It's spelled, "TerreEnce" for the record.)

One particular Father's day twelve years after he had passed, while arguing with my wife I stormed out of the house with our son Hendrix and drove around for a while to calm down and realized I needed to bury the hatchet once and for all. I knew I couldn't walk back into the house the same person because things would only get worse.

Becoming drastically desperate, I took our youngest son with me to my dad's grave. I needed him for extra motivation to **face** my inner demons. About 45 minutes later I finally get there. I walk inside the front office and asked about the location of my father's headstone. Can you imagine the embarrassment? The lady asked who I was and if there was any relation. I told her I was his son and she said: "Boy, don't let this be the last time I see you here." I slowly pulled up to his grave and I'm left with the option to chicken out like I've always done or to make an example to my son who looks up to me.

So I gathered my thoughts and made a quick confessional video to upload onto my old YouTube channel and got out the car. "None of this feels real." I kept telling myself. I've played this exact scenario in my head a million times but nothing was quite like being **face** to **face** with my dad's headstone.

Even though he wasn't physically there to talk to I apologized for holding back how I felt and never addressing my pain and frustration. I remember it raining briefly and I couldn't move, I cried and held onto my son until I had nothing left to say to my dad.

I went back in my car, did another confessional video to upload and finally took a deep sigh of relief. Twelve years of weight was left behind, I had **finish**ed that chapter in my life and could come home and be the husband and father that my dad could have never been.

Look, perhaps your life is a construction zone right now. Maybe you've got orange cones and yellow tape all around your obstacles. Yes, it's gonna hurt but you'll always suffer if you can't progress past the pain. Not until you **face** it. Life will keep punishing you and pushing you and when your back is up against the wall you can only move one way and that's forward that's why I need you to **finish** it!

The last three years of my dad's life I robbed him of his fatherhood. I asked him for some money and he hung up on me I was angry, upset and ashamed. I'd even block his calls, there was a time when I once I changed his name on my phone to "do not answer". One morning before waking up for work, my mom called me and told me he had a heart attack and died suddenly. I brushed it off, I never **faced** it I never dealt with it. Until I almost lost my wife and my family.

WHAT'S FACING IT?
Going toe to toe with the obstacle

WHAT'S FINISHING IT?
Leaving the obstacle at your mercy

Every question on this test of life you take should be like a punch to your obstacles **face**, it's time to **finish** it fatality mode like in the classic game Mortal Kombat.

THE I WANNA'S:
- You wanna lose weight but you refuse to step on the scale
- You wanna get good grades and make your parents proud but your mouth is open and your books are closed

- You wanna leave that miserable job but you stay stuck on repetitive behavior
- You wanna keep avoiding that check up but don't know if something's wrong with you

SHAKE THINGS UP

Sometimes in life, you gotta shake things up, dealing with my anger forced me to remember what I currently had and most importantly what I could have lost. This is why I love snow globes because there's symbolism in them. When you first see a snow globe it's not moving, everything has settled to the bottom. But you gotta pick it up, shake it up, take action, and as a result, it creates a beautiful situation. You see it's the process that makes things wonderful and that's what everyone loves.

You just have to make sure that you're in control of what's being shaken. Because debt can shake you, losing your job can shake you, a divorce can shake you. Be mindful so that you can land in the desired destiny. If you aren't happy where you're currently are, you must evaluate and shake things up.

TERRENCE'S TAKEAWAY

WHAT YOU DESERVE GETS EXPOSED TO YOU WITH EVERY PROGRESSIVE ATTEMPT YOU MAKE TO DESTROY COMFORT.

A GRUDGE IS NOTHING BUT MASKED SABOTAGE.

IF YOU STAY ATTACHED TO THE OBSTACLE YOU CAN'T EVER LET GO OF SOMETHING AND ALLOW ROOM TO GROW AND HEAL.

ACTION IS THE SUPERPOWER THAT ATTRACTS AND MAGNETIZES OPPORTUNITY.

YOUR TAKEAWAYS:

WHAT WILL YOU FACE & FINISH?

YOUR EXCUSES CARRY A CURRENCY AND NOT INCOME IS GOOD. HAVE YOUR EXCUSES PAID FOR YOUR CURRENT SETBACK?

I DON'T AIM TO BE THE WORLD'S GREATEST SPEAKER, M ONLY GOAL IS FOR YOU TO DESTROY THE UNDERACHIEVER.

CHAPTER 5
CHOOSE YOUR WEAPON

"Without action, your setbacks hold no expiration."

You can **face** your obstacles empty handed or with a weapon. What's the difference between a quick fix and a major problem? Quick fixes usually justify minor problems. But what if you couldn't solve the issue by yourself and you needed reinforcement? Some problems are bigger than you see and will require wisdom you don't currently have, the discomfort you haven't yet experienced or an outside eye to see yourself.

When I was in middle school I wanted to be a professional bowler. I guess I was always attracted to the idea of being presented with something heavy to attack the obstacles with. I looked at bowling as therapeutic. My concentration had to be just as heavy as any ball I used. It's good to have values, morals, and overall intentions.

As crazy as it sounds, I actually tell people not to buy my books quite often. Why would I do that? Simple, not everyone is qualified to read them. Now I'm not saying that to sound cocky. But I didn't spend 3 to 4 years writing something to sit on someone's shelf or to not be implemented.

You'll say everything on your mind to a coworker but not to your boss. You'll nit-pick about your spouse to a friend but won't say it to your significant other. Or feel as if you're broke but consistently work to buy new and shiny stuff just to replace the prior stuff. People unsubscribe from my emails every day and say that I e-mail too much. But it just solidifies the people who value what I bring to the table.

Weapon # 1: Change

If you don't have what you want, the reason may be because you don't currently deserve it. I'm not saying this to offend you, or to make you feel some type of way. But if you're still yearning and haven't laid an actionable trail, perhaps you simply aren't qualified to acquire or take on what you feel you deserve. This problem is more common than people are willing to admit.

How do you solve this? Put an expiration date on your setbacks and goals. When I wrote my first book my goal was to be published before our daughter was born. The exact date of my goal was 12/31/17, as my luck or lack thereof would have it our daughter was born on December 27th.

Weapon # 2: Words

Don't ever attempt to diminish the power of spoken word. Even as an author I guess I underestimated the power words have. I recently attended a book expo and as people approached my table with interest I heard the word "need" almost consistently.

"my daughter NEEDS this"
"my son NEEDS this"
"my husband NEEDS this"

I'm not saying this to boast, but to inform you that your words are more powerful externally then you could ever imagine them to be. There's a reason why my ancestors were forbidden to read.

Recently a customer bought a book and informed me that her son needed (there's that word again) to read it, he had recently gone through a nasty divorce and had even become suicidal. As heavy as it sounds, it was even heavier knowing this person in that particular mindset would be reading my thoughts, ideas, and lessons on paper.

You have the knowledge that will impact, entertain and possibly save someone's life. We as a generation can't progress by keeping thoughts and ideas to ourselves. Remember that the weight of your words are not measured by your thoughts, but by how others are affected by what you have to say.

There's someone in this world, in your inner circle who needs to hear what you have to say. What's holding you back? You pack a punch to impact the world internally.

Weapon #4: Empty hands

Let go or be dragged. It's funny how losing weight is one of the most sought after goals we have. Weight loss requires two main things: eating healthy and working out. Yet in our everyday lives, we take on and **face** so many projects, tasks, and jobs that require much more than a simple two-step process.

Look at the house or building you're in right now. The computer, laptop or cell phone you're reading this on, marriage, raising children or teenagers and even driving. What's my point? Let's work on the quality of our efforts with the things we come in contact with. Hey, I'm not perfect I'm working on this as we speak!

Weapon #5: Books

Often in life, we overlook the power of a book, your book is a transformation device. Such as using a knife or fork to eat. They are no different than the books we use to feed our brains.

Weapon # 6: Purification

It's been said, "*What's done in the dark will eventually come to light*" Today will soon be over. One afternoon our son had his shoes in the living room and I asked him not to just pick them up but I told him to put them where they belong because the house was a mess. Then he responded with "why dada why do things get messy?" It's always because we don't put things back where they belong, we get comfortable.

I want you to think of the setbacks, obstacles and bad habits you've just simply passed over and swept under the rug. What have you cleaned up today?

Weapon # 7: People
Recently, our son suggested I read Curious George or (Monkey George as he likes to say). Curious George spilled grape juice on the floor (Most children's books usually have a problem and a purpose)

George tried to do what any normal person would, by instantly trying to fix the situation. He grabs a bunch of paper towels and realizes it isn't making the problem any better so he suddenly remembers that soap is good for cleaning.

He grabs a hose from outside thinking it would surely clean up the grape juice, but he created an even bigger problem than just spilling the juice. He got so much water into the house that he needed to use a neighbor's water pump to remove the excess water. What's the lesson in all this? Well, have you ever tried to fix a problem only to make it worse? We all have.

While we can't wait and sit on the problems in life there comes a time where we must ask others for help. Next time you get on social media understand you're probably connected with someone who may have gone through what you've gone through and wouldn't mind giving you their two cents. Just remember, it's the ones listening and asking the questions that have the power.

Weapon # 8: Penetration

Bruce Lee said he doesn't fear a man who knows 10,000 kicks but the man who has mastered one kick 10,000 times. Let me tell you something about trying to hit your target and what made Bruce Lee the greatest martial artist to ever live. Bruce didn't just see targets on the sur**face** level.. When he aimed at a target he aimed 3 to 4 inches past where the target literally was.

Stop aiming to hit, start aiming to penetrate. Who cares if you just simply hit your goals? Penetrate them. Leave a mark so imprinted that the person or obstacle that comes after you has to know what you did to get the job done.

WITHOUT ACTION, YOUR SETBACKS HOLD NO EXPIRATION.

IT'S CRAZY HOW WE COMPLAIN AND REMAIN THE SAME.

GOALS ARE "CUTE" BUT IF YOUR CURRENT EFFORTS CAN'T RUN CIRCLES AROUND YOUR PAST HABITS, WHAT DOES THAT SAY ABOUT THE DURATION IT'LL TAKE TO ACTUALLY GET TO YOUR DESIRED RESULTS?

WE AS HUMANS ARE WALKING, TALKING LIBRARIES.

IT ISN'T THE AMOUNT OF STEPS YOU TAKE TO GET TO THE OUTCOME, IT'S THE QUALITY AND DISCIPLINE YOU IMPLEMENT.

YOUR TAKEAWAYS:

WHAT WILL YOU FACE & FINISH?

YOUR EXCUSES CARRY A CURRENCY AND NOT INCOME IS GOOD. HAVE YOUR EXCUSES PAID FOR YOUR CURRENT SETBACK?

CHAPTER 6
FACE IT

"Some things you just can't put in the microwave."

I recently traded in my 2004 Scion XB or "box car" for an SUV. (You can call me a soccer dad if you wish). No matter how smooth I tried to look in my Scion, no matter how much money was in my pocket, no matter how high of a level my swag was on, I still had to **face** the fact that I needed to open up the back door, reach around to the drivers side and unlock the front door to get inside.

With a growing family, two baby seats in the back and a car that wouldn't legally pass inspection. I knew I had waited long enough. I needed something safer for my family and myself. My mother and wife would often tell me for years how I needed a new car, but I made a personal goal to be in a new car by December 31st, 2018. I wanted an outcome so bad that I **face**d the problem and created a result.

My wife had spoken to the car salesman hours before I had arrived at the lot. I decided to look right after I got off of work and seconds after I arrived, the salesman pulled up with exactly what I needed. I knew

I wanted the car before I had even gotten inside. The offer I received was slap yo mama ridiculous and my family left with the SUV that night. You see, I wouldn't have allowed myself this opportunity if it wasn't for me letting go of I was afraid to **face**. The thought of my insurance going up, allowing my credit score to take a hit and a car note with an already limited income paralyzed my opportunity to see, think and live a better experience.

THE BUS MINDSET

A bus is generally open to the public, anybody can get on, it's big, moves much slower than a car and people ride together but they're going to different destinations.

THE CAR MINDSET

Cars are much lighter and faster they don't have as much weighing it down which allows it to get to the point of destination much faster. Cars have limited seating not everyone can get in and everyone inside is typically going to the same destination.

GET SPECIFIC

Some things you just can't put in the microwave. Sometimes you gotta go through something crazy to get to something amazing.

Recently a friend of mine apologized for the brief absence she had given me, she said "sorry I'm just going through a lot right now". So my response was "Alright, when do you plan on getting there?" Without airing her dirty laundry, I thought to myself there are two ways of looking at this:

1. She's more "stuck" than anything
2. That short little handicap of a statement "I'm going through a lot" we've all said it. But what does it really mean?

To go "through" something there must first be a start and end point. When you say you've got a lot going on and you're going through a lot, are you evaluating how you got into the spot you're at now? Do you have a destination in mind?

Because maybe you're not only stuck where you are, perhaps you've made a home and settled in it as well. Especially if you lack a desire for a game plan. If you have multiple obstacles going on in your life you gotta take care of them one by one. You can't leave one race to go **finish** another one, with this mindset you'll often leave things undone creating a cycle of more work for yourself and more stress. So stop telling yourself "I'm going through a lot" and actually go through the issues. Have a destination in mind and keep moving towards completion.

ADDRESS THE ISSUE

My goal is to change the way you think about that

particular phrase by flipping and dissecting your current paradigm.

HERE ARE SOME EXAMPLES:

YOUR BOSS: I've noticed the past several weeks you've been clocking in late to work.
YOU: Sorry I'm just going through a lot right now.

YOUR CHILDREN: Our internet's down I thought you paid the bill?
YOU: Sorry I'm just going through a lot right now.

YOUR SPOUSE: Our son's temperature is not going down, did you remember to give him any medicine?
YOU: Sorry I'm just going through a lot right now

These are all excuses. Do you see how the result of not taking action is addressed first, then followed with the excuse?

Toilet paper, batteries, food, hygiene products, gas, doors. These are all things you actually go through. Often when we say we're going through something we have no game plan to get out of where we currently are. We say we're going through something but really we're actually stuck.

For Christmas, our oldest son Hezekiah got a basketball goal and I ironically received a 128 piece tool set (thanks Santa). I spent over four hours outside trying to get the goal set up properly. I left the incomplete goal in the backyard for a week. Not realizing that I'd have to look at it every time we ate at the dining table or went into the living room. I was stuck! Our son went away for the weekend and I promised myself when he'd get home he'd have a basketball goal all set up for him. Another five hours later it was done.

The entire time I was literally working on a goal (pun intended). It was all symbolism in order to make a goal you must take action. Instead of saying "I'm going through something" know that you're really going through excuses and a lack of action. You're only getting further away and sinking even deeper.

What is it that you're really going through and have you set up checkpoints? Mile markers? The plan to address this is pretty black and white you have to confront the elephant in the room. You're stuck on the excuse.

While I wont disclose the exact institution of my previous employer, let's just say I worked at a Cancer hospital. Not just any cancer hospital but the biggest one in the world that just so happens to be in one of the fattest cities in the United States. I'll never forget, it was September 11th. No, not the day the planes supposedly hit the Twin Towers this was the year of

2015. Have you ever had to take on multiple tasks at once? Or perform a balancing act for hire if you will. Ever feel like an octopus?

We had a team and if any member of the team was sick or on vacation, their job duties would spread out onto our worklist. The goal was to **finish** the assigned work before the coworker returns, it didn't always happen but it was always the intention.

This particular Monday morning, my coworker came back from vacation to additional work on her list. She wasn't a happy camper and felt the need to express that to me, without any filtration or hesitation. The email that I had received was so disrespectful that if I were to respond with even a quarter of the disrespect I would instantly be fired. How do I know? I confirmed it with our supervisor who agreed with that exact statement.

What's one to do at this moment? What would you do? Dish it out the same way it was given to you? Let your coworker get away with it? Or report it to your manager? Believe me, I wanted to tell her how I felt about her: mother, father and even her dog as a whole. But as I said before, we were a team and I had a pregnant girlfriend at the time so by default I was forced to choose my next steps very carefully.

Knowing that if I didn't correct this in a

professional manner right then and there then I'd risk the chance of this recurring in the future and perhaps while I'm not so mentally calm or collective. I simply forwarded the email to our supervisor and asked how to handle this matter. She gladly offered to submit a request with our manager to schedule a departmental group meeting with human resources. Thinking that was the absolute best scenario available, due to the fact that everyone on our team would have a fair chance of speaking and addressing any obstructions or provide possible resolutions.

A couple of days went by and words hadn't been exchanged between this coworker and myself. But I did happen to catch our manager discussing Monday's ordeal with my coworker. Immediately I felt a storm brewing, why? Because the whole purpose of the group meeting was so that everyone could have a fair opportunity to speak and eliminate drama not to verbally bash each other. Was I ever called into the office by our manager to discuss how I felt? Of course not. Our manager put herself in a position to obtain an opinion before I ever had the opportunity to utter a word about the situation to her.

Perhaps you may be thinking "Terrence grow up and stop being such a baby". Well, this wouldn't be my first time in this situation from a manager. I learned from a previous employer at a psych hospital that it's best to document and document I did. Building up until this altercation, I had a physical file with twenty-seven pages of documented proof in which I was treated differently from other coworkers in situations. Three days after this problem, my manager called me into her office. I think to myself "Great! I get an opportunity to speak."

Thirty seconds after I entered the office, my manager's manager enters the office. So I think to myself, "ok is THIS how I'm going to get fired?" Out came a white sheet of paper from our manager's desk. This paper was a screenshot of a **Face**book post I had made several months ago. Like many others, at the time I'd often use social media to vent. This particular post stated: "My manager is always so quick to put people in their own place, it feels good to finally make her smell her own shit." Out of my entire **Face**book friends list I only had one actual coworker, leaving the process of elimination quite simple. My job didn't have access to my social media accounts and my account was set so that anyone who wasn't my friend couldn't see any of my information.

The coworker who I was friends with on **Face**book just so happened to share the same office as... yes you guessed it. The same lady I was having the issue with. My only defense to both manager's was that I was working two jobs and had two managers. (Which was true, I was a personal trainer at the time.) So just because she saw the post it didn't officially mean it was about her. They both said ok and I was sent back to continue working.

I took my work keys off of my keychain and started cleaning up. Why? I knew the odds were against me. Two days later I was terminated for something completely bogus and unrelated. I was let go for restricting a patient's approval to be seen due to non-authorization. Little did I know that my manager had made a undocumated verbal agreement for this particular patient to be seen first and obtain any authorizations later.

I followed protocol and played fair. A week later I was denied unemployment. With a lack of consistent income, I found myself at a job fair, less than a week after I accepted a job paying $12 an hour. I had to **face** it.

TERRENCE'S TAKEAWAY

THE WORLD WILL SHOW IT'S ASS ONCE YOU DECIDE TO PLACE A DATE ON WHAT YOU AIM TO ACCOMPLISH.

IN ORDER TO GO THROUGH SOMETHING, YOU MUST HAVE A DESTINATION IN MIND.

THERE'S A BIG DIFFERENCE BETWEEN RESOLVING THE ISSUE AND ABANDONING THE OBSTACLE.

YOUR TAKEAWAYS:

WHAT WILL YOU FACE & FINISH?

STOP GIVING THE CLOCK AWAY TO PEOPLE THAT WANNA WASTE YOUR TIME.

IT'S HARD TO HEAR YOUR ASPIRATIONS SCREAMING IF YOUR EARS ARE PLUGGED WITH EXCUSES

TERRENCE SANI - 88

CHAPTER 7
FINISH IT

"How many times have you started something with the best of intentions?"

Why can't you get things done? Too often I hear "I'm overwhelmed" but you aren't actually overwhelmed, it's your lack of application that defaults you to underachieve and miss your target. If you're overwhelmed you're not on solid ground which means your foundation is faulty. You're overwhelmed because you got in your own way. What should irritate you even more is the fact that we're never taught what "overwhelmed" really even means if anything.

Whelmed - engulf, submerge or bury.

So let's break this down a little bit. Now that you know the definition of whelmed please understand that something that's already past its peak can't suddenly become overdue, you can't kill what's already dead and that you can't overpour something that's already spilling or has been spilled.

The triple C's (Contain, command and complete)
Often times in life we feel like we aren't where we feel we need to be. It's likely due to the fact that we

contain our problems instead of commanding and completing them. There are times when we beat ourselves up and dwell on the lack of a better situation. We default to being the victim, burying any paths whatsoever that leads to becoming a victor. But who respects that? How actionable is feeling sorry for yourself? Do you have a manager or supervisor at work who simply separates themselves when it comes to challenges? If so, are they highly respected? Can you depend on them to get the job done?

What if you took the command and complete approach? People in high positions obtain greatness because they moved out of the contain stage. Successful people get things done. It's that simple. You don't need me to tell you that things will not always go right but you do need to understand that when you begin to command, your intentions start to suddenly become aligned to help you complete the task.

Stop and flop

How many times have you started something with the best of intentions? Creating Youtube videos, reading daily, posting blogs, working out, eating healthy, ect. Only to phase out after a few days or a week. Has this ever happened to you before? Success is more often a momentum game. It's proceeded by the steps taken prior.

Even as a speaker I've noticed if I go a few days without posting something motivational on social media, a few days without reaching out to prospective clients or even a week or two without surrounding myself around positive people, and following up on upcoming events, my momentum for getting booked starts to decline.

This world is competitive, people are in search of the next new and upcoming shiny, little or big thing. Everyone is waiting for the latest and greatest phone. The freshest exclusive celebrity endorsed sneakers. We live for the upgrades while downgrading our level of execution. If you stop or slow down you'll get buried in competition. If you stop you'll flop. So you want to continue having success correct? Start applying your ability to **face** and **finish** things into all areas of your life!

Resiliency

At home I never saw the point in keeping up with our grass, all I'd ever do was cut it. Did I water it? Hell no, I let mother nature take care of that and waited until it rained. My mother was always quick to tell me how other yards in the neighborhood looked and how bad ours was. Eventually, I realized it's much more than the look of maintaining your grass. It's a representation of how well you take care of yourself.

How are you going to master a big obstacle if you

can't master something so small? How you do anything is how you do everything. Don't take care of something in your life just because someone else is watching. Treat your purpose as if no one is there at all. Grass needs sunlight to grow but if you give it too much more than it can handle.. guess what? It'll burn.

After I'd cut the grass it would look good for a few days but a week later it was back to looking like trash. That's because it wasn't treated. Untreated weeds are resilient, untreated habits are resilient, untreated behavior is resilient. Water your thirst for knowledge obtain the right food to feed your purpose.

TERRENCE'S TAKEAWAY

WHAT ARE YOUR ACTIONABLE DEFAULTS? (BOTH GOOD AND BAD)

ARE YOU TRYING TO FIX WHAT'S ALREADY RESOLVED?

ARE YOU CURRENTLY ON AN EXPEDITION TO DISCOVER SOMETHING NEW BECAUSE YOU AREN'T CONTENT AND REFUSE TO ACCEPT THE UNFILTERED VERSION OF WHAT YOU FOUND OR THE WAY THINGS ACTUALLY ARE?

WHY DO YOU FEEL THE NEED TO CONTINUE SCRATCHING A RESOLVED ITCH?

YOUR TAKEAWAYS:

WHAT WILL YOU

FACE & FINISH?

I DON'T AIM TO BE THE WORLD'S GREATEST SPEAKER, MY ONLY GOAL IS FOR YOU TO DESTROY THE UNDERACHIEVER.

CHAPTER 8
ELIMINATE REOCCURRENCES

"An unwanted force could result in a relapse of the intended goal."

I bet you believe you can do whatever it takes to succeed. But it's that exact word "whatever" that's holding you back. Why? The word "whatever" is a pretty muddy way to handle a specific situation. The word whatever gives you artificial permission to create a map to success. But you can't possibly know which direction to go until you get naked. (Have no fear, this rest of this section is still PG-13)

When our youngest son Hendrix was born I was told by the nurse to spend as much chest to chest skin to skin time with him as possible. Hendrix had to learn and adapt to everything I had to offer.

success doesn't know your heartbeat
success doesn't know what you smell like
success doesn't know what you look like
success doesn't know your voice
You've gotta **bare it all and make it known!**

If you don't want to deal with the same recurring issues and problems you must be willing to remove all of the layers between you and your obstacles. So I need you to ask yourself, are you willing to be vulnerable? If you don't **face** it and **finish** the problem or goal someone else will complete the job for you. They might not do as sweet of a job as you but it doesn't matter if you've already forfeited your opportunity by quitting.

As a matter of fact, you made the reward that much sweeter by putting the responsibility in the hands of someone else. To you, the action of quitting appears to be silent but quitting actually screams out to others as "here's an opportunity and I've already done some of the work for you".

We've all had a mess to clean up whether it was our own or someone else's. It's something we often dread because it takes away from what we would rather be doing. But no matter the type of mess that's plaguing you it never created itself just as an obstacle never presents itself without a lesson and opportunity. Know that lack of action is actually an action within itself. Things get messy because you refuse to put things where they belong. It's time to clean up!

It's been said that if you think about it too much you'll never get it done. But what really holds us back is the risk, we need to and want to narrow that window of risk. Where there is risk, there isn't a guaranteed solidified outcome which hinders us. Don't depend on what you don't have. IOU's can't grow your business or make you successful. I wanna's and I'm gonna's aren't forms of currency. People will want to help, advise and sell you on something. I suggest you bet on yourself before you put all the weight on someone else.

"Just one more"

I came across a common handicap that's usually a gateway to keep you stuck. This is pretty EPIC but also common. No matter how far you want to progress in life or simply give up a bad habit, there's ONE simple statement that'll hold you back and possibly push you further into depression, jealousy and defeat.

How many times have you used the following phrase(s):

I'll see him/her *just one more* time
Just one more slice of cheesecake
Just one more drink
Just one more hit
I'll do you a favor *just this one last* time..

This is a HORRIBLE game plan to attack any obstacle. You're up to 50% more likely to go back (or stay committed) to setbacks by relying on this particular mindset.

Try changing your "one more time" to "the first day"

This is *the FIRST day* I won't allow anyone to get the best of me.

This is *the FIRST day* I won't eat unhealthy foods.

This is *the FIRST day* I won't involve myself in negativity and bad relationships.

This is the FIRST day I'll bring acknowledgment and awareness to what's holding me back.

Changing unsatisfied situations

You may work a job you absolutely hate, you may look at your bank account and not be satisfied with what you see. You could be in a relationship and arguing, struggling and fighting and the other person just won't let it go.

How do you get over that?
How do you get past it?
How do you change it?

You don't and you can't. You don't have the power to change anyone but yourself. However the actions and ideas you display can spark the person to want to change themselves and their behavior.

If your job sucks it most likely won't change. If you look at your bank balance and you're unhappy with what you see because there are more transitions going out than going in. The only thing that you can change is YOU.

If you change yourself, that relationship will possibly change. Maybe they'll see something inside themselves and be inspired by the changes you've made. You have to put yourself in a situation where you no longer have to be in a taxing environment anymore. Then you no longer have to deal with negativity. If you *really* hate your job you'll find another one.

You don't stop a drug addict by asking them to stop. You stop them by planting a seed and allowing the user to want to stop themselves. Unwanted force could result in a relapse of the intended goal.

TERRENCE'S TAKEAWAY

STOP SAYING AND DISPLAYING HOW COMFORTABLE YOU ARE.

PEOPLE ARE LOOKING TO EXECUTE ON YOUR LEFTOVERS.

NEVER UNDERESTIMATE THE POWER OF NOW.

BE A RESULT TO INSPIRE A CHANGE.

YOUR TAKEAWAYS:

WHAT WILL YOU FACE & FINISH?

IT CAN'T BE
THAT BAD IF
YOU'RE
GOING BACK
TO IT
EVERYDAY.

DIVORCE YOUR MARRIAGE TO EXCUSES, TAKE INTEGRITY OUT ON A DATE.

TERRENCE SANI – 106

CHAPTER 9
REMEMBER YOUR WOUNDS

"Opportunity comes from effort not excuses."

As lazy as people may seem to be you'd be surprised, they'll almost never put themselves in a position to starve. Why? Because those hunger pains never go away until some type of action is taken. People get desperate, and when you're hungry and can't physically see the next meal.. you'll do just about anything you can to get to the next step, even if it's unjust. My wife has to work weekends which means less time with our family. That hurts. Too often we look to heal our wounds without realizing how to eliminate them from reoccurring.

I lost but I won

A few years ago, I won second place in a Toastmasters speech contest against a guy with over seven years of experience. Pay close attention to how I worded that. Why didn't I say I lost? Check this out.. During his interview, he said I was his influence, on top of that he wanted to introduce me to his inner circle. He said I have a message the whole world needs to hear and that he has no idea how I got second place.

So did I really lose or did I win? Often we wanna "hustle hard" and have tunnel vision. We think linear when we come up short because we lack the ability to see the good things that come.. not from a win or loss but from simply effort alone.

If you're making an "effort" you can't really ever come up short. How would your spouse feel if you just consistently made an effort at putting a smile on their **face**? If you made an effort in school, with finances, with your weight, ect.

Opportunity comes from "effort", not excuses. What efforts have you made today?

Resistance

Stop saying it's hard and start saying it's necessary. You might be in the wrong profession, you may need to be a personal trainer or bodybuilder. Why? Because every time you say something's "hard" you mentally add resistance to the actual thing you're trying to do. You go to work and say it's hard so you go into work with that additional resistance on top of you. Perhaps you'd like to lose weight and you constantly say it's so hard to lose because nothing's coming off. You make eating the right food that much more difficult. You make that workout session that much more difficult. If you're in a relationship and you complain and say it's too hard, it makes the relationship that much harder trust me.

Start saying it's necessary:

"I go to work because it's necessary that I provide for my family." That's what makes it a tad easier to get to point b. Wanna build a business? Start saying it's necessary. You'll come to find that the necessary steps you need to take will start presenting themselves.

TERRENCE'S TAKEAWAY

YOU KNOW WHAT YOU MUST FACE

YOU KNOW WHY YOU MUST FACE IT

I'VE HELPED YOU BUILD A MAP, NOW IT'S UP TO YOU TO TAKE ON THE JOURNEY AND PENETRATE UNTIL YOU REACH THE DESTINATION.

YOUR STRUGGLE IS SMALLER THAN YOUR ABILITY TO SUCCEED.

YOUR TAKEAWAYS:

WHAT WILL YOU FACE & FINISH?

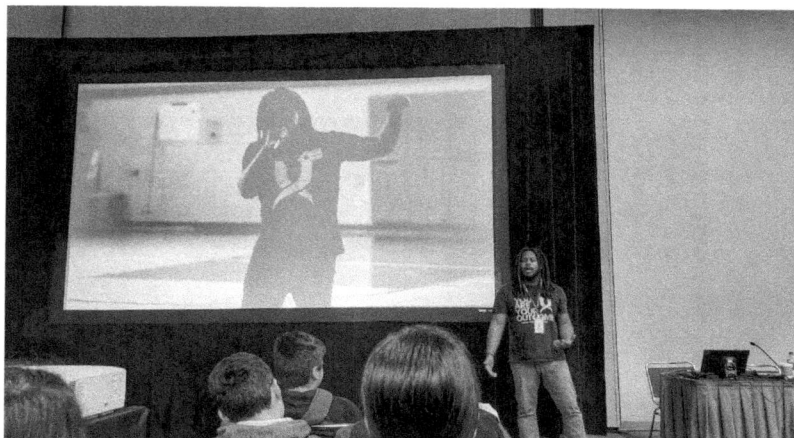

ABOUT THE AUTHOR

"In one week I faced the sudden death of my step dad, an anniversary, funeral, birthday and proposal."

When catastrophic things happen in your life you can't help but naturally self-evaluate your current way of living. Everyday life was telling me I had a purpose. Each excuse buries who you want to be, where you want to go and diminishes your drive. I majored in procrastination, pink slips (both termination and late notice letters), pushing priorities to the limit and stretching deadlines out as much as possible. I even took time getting out of the womb, my birthday is the last day of the year (December 31st).

My step father passed away suddenly in his sleep. I was so comfortable with him being alive that I never thought of death. I was so comfortable that I didn't know my life was built on the foundation of a rug that could get pulled from beneath me at any given moment. I was **face** to **face** with a man whose wishes, goals and intentions all had an expiration date.

Previous books from the author:

Don't unify yourself with what you lack, welcome what you aim to evolve.

YOU ARE YOUR OUTCOME

HOW TO ELIMINATE SELF-MADE OBSTACLES, SETBACKS AND FEAR

TERRENCE SANI

Order today at:
YouAreYourOutcome.com

Student Development:

Helping your students expire excuses!

Do your students suffer with both self and academic confidence? Let's reduce your dropout rates and increase classroom performance. Let's turn student obstacles into outcomes.

Here's how we can help:

Speaking

If it's a classroom, auditorium or one on one.. Terrence WILL put you in a position to protest your comfort zone.

Coaching

1 on 1 with your most challenging students. Teaching them how to remove all the noise and get focused.

Lunch & learn

A unique learning experience with breakout sessions & activities that focus on communication and comprehension.

FOR BOOKING: HELLO@TERRENCESANI.COM

Personal & Professional Development:

Learn how to bulldoze any setbacks you've created that stop you from getting the outcome you deserve and how to redirect fear to maximize opportunity.

Terrence Sani is a true advocate who speaks the importance of discovering who you are and associating yourself with your life's purpose. Terrence builds your confidence to go toe to toe with excuses and obstacles until you win. While many bury setbacks in misery, he shows that success is the sum of consistent effort. Take action today and you won't have to suffer tomorrow.

FOR BOOKING: HELLO@TERRENCESANI.COM

Subscribe to the brand new podcast!

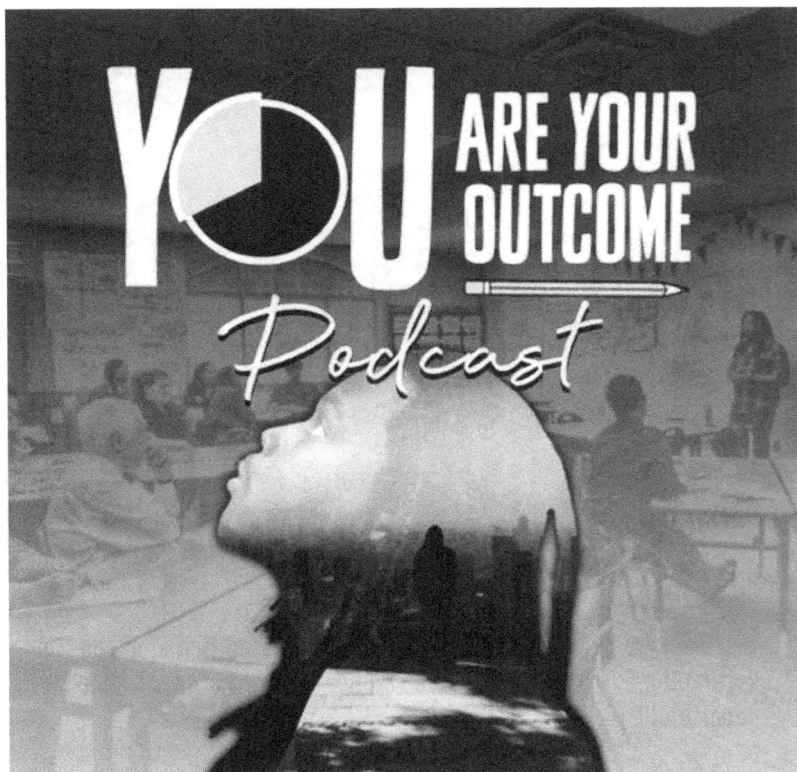

Anchor.fm/terrence-sani

Thank You

Facebook: TerrenceSani1 **Instagram:** TerrenceSani

www.ingramcontent.com/pod-product-compliance
Lightning Source LLC
LaVergne TN
LVHW051249080426
835513LV00016B/1825